First World War
and Army of Occupation
War Diary
France, Belgium and Germany

5 DIVISION
Divisional Troops
Divisional Anti-Gas School
1 April 1918 - 31 March 1919

WO95/1539/4

The Naval & Military Press Ltd
www.nmarchive.com
Published in association with The National Archives

Published by

The Naval & Military Press Ltd

Unit 10 Ridgewood Industrial Park,

Uckfield, East Sussex,

TN22 5QE England

Tel: +44 (0) 1825 749494

www.naval-military-press.com

www.nmarchive.com

This diary has been reprinted in facsimile from the original. Any imperfections are inevitably reproduced and the quality may fall short of modern type and cartographic standards.

© **Crown Copyright**
Images reproduced by permission of The National Archives, London, England, 2015.

Contents

Document type	Place/Title	Date From	Date To
Heading	WO95/1539/4		
Heading	5th Division Anti Gas School 1918 Apr 1919 Mar I Gas Service H.Q		
War Diary	In The Field	01/04/1918	30/04/1918
Heading	War Diary of 5th Divn Anti Gas School For Month Of May 1918		
War Diary	In The Field	01/05/1918	31/05/1918
Heading	War Diary of 5th Divl Anti Gas School For Month Of June1918		
War Diary	In The Field	01/06/1918	30/06/1918
Heading	War Diary of 5th Div Anti Gas School Month Of July 1918		
War Diary	In The Field	01/07/1918	31/07/1918
Heading	War Diary of 5th Div Gas Officer For Month Of August 1918		
War Diary	In The Field	01/08/1918	31/08/1918
Heading	War Diary of 5th Div Anti Gas School For Month Of September 1918		
War Diary	In The Field	01/09/1918	30/09/1918
Heading	War Diary of Gas Services 5th Division For Month Of October 1918		
War Diary	In The Field	01/10/1918	31/10/1918
Heading	War Diary of Gas Services 5th Div For Month Of November 1918.		
War Diary	In The Field	01/11/1918	30/11/1918
Heading	War Diary of Gas Services 5th Div For Month Of December 1918		
War Diary	In The Field	01/12/1918	31/12/1918
Heading	War Diary of Gas Services Headquarters 5 Division January 1st 1919 To January 31st 1919		
War Diary	Rhisnes	01/01/1919	31/01/1919
Heading	War Diary of Gas Services 5 Division From 1.2.19 To 28.2.19.		
War Diary	Rhisnes	01/02/1919	28/02/1919
Heading	War Diary of Gas Services, 5 Division From 1st March 1919 To 31st March 1919		
War Diary	Rhisnes	01/03/1919	16/03/1919
War Diary	Gembloux	17/03/1919	31/03/1919

WO 95/15394

5th Division

Anti Gas School,

~~January~~ TO ~~December~~
APRIL
1918
1918 APR — 1919 MAR
& Gas Services, H.Q,

(ITALY)

Army Form C. 2118.

WAR DIARY
or
INTELLIGENCE SUMMARY

(Erase heading not required.) of 5" Divl. Gas Officer

Place	Date	Hour	Summary of Events and Information	Remarks and references to Appendices
In the Field	1.4.18 to 8.4.18		D.G.O. and Staff entrained at POZANA for journey to France on the 2nd inst., and detrained at MONDICOURT & G.H.Q. Officers and Stores fixed at LUCHEUX.	
	9.4.18 to 11.4.18		D.G.O. visited C.C.A. VI Corps and various Units. Routine work by Adv. Gas H.Q. and at Corps. Bde Gas Books replaced by P.G.O. Received orders to move at 24 hrs notice.	
	12.4.18		Move from LUCHEUX to AIRE. D.G.O. on motor cycle. Staff returns by lorry.	
	13.4.18 to 15.4.18		D.G.O. visited C.C.A. at FONTES, Div.H.Q. and the three Bde H.Qs re L. training of reinforcements coming to abnormal demands for replacements. D.G.O. borrowed 450 S.B.Rs from 61st Divn. Fresh Bde Bks & D.G.E.S.	
	16.4.18 to 19.4.18		D.G.O. visited various units of 95th Bde re condition of S.B.Rs and 39th C.C.S. re S.B.R. Cross 2491 forms 12th Bde were sent to 15th Bde H.Q. pending the return of Sgt. Hogarth. Kaphus Work at Bde and at dispersal	
	20.4.18 to 21.4.18		D.G.O. visited D.H.Q. Bde Hdqrs and functions in Foret de Nieppe. Arrangements made for safety of cadre of units in the supp. Units. Were Lts O.R.s M & NCOs at 8 % of II NCOs at 18 % of men in Gas shelled areas. Report received of contaminated Gas clothing on the div. front. Various areas in Foret de Nieppe gas-shelled.	
	22.4.18		D.G.O., C.C.A. & F.A. Langwill visited Gas shelled areas in Foret de Nieppe. 1st D.C.L.I., 12th Gloucs., 11th R. Sk. R. and R.A.M.C. Reports sent to C.C.A. and to G.S.O.II and 1st Field Amb. to water report in ground card.	
	23.4.18 to 24.4.18		D.G.O. visited Army H.Q. Gas Sgt. Hogart returned from leave and rejoined & D.G.O. Adv. Gas Depot reported at 1.5 T.O.T. re Gas shelled areas and measures taken to counteract the effects of the "Mustard" Gas. Reports sent to C.C.A.	
	25.4.18		D.G.O. visited Gassed areas in Foret de Nieppe occupied by 1/1st O.C.A. & 1st D.C.L.I. Fs. Arrangements made for maintenance of Chloride of Lime Dumps at critical locations, provision of Special towelettes, and supply of "Gloves" for use in dealing with Gassed clothing etc.	

Army Form C. 2118.

WAR DIARY
or
INTELLIGENCE SUMMARY
(Erase heading not required.) 5th Division / Gas Officer

Instructions regarding War Diaries and Intelligence Summaries are contained in F.S. Regs., Part II. and the Staff Manual respectively. Title pages will be prepared in manuscript.

Place	Date	Hour	Summary of Events and Information	Remarks and references to Appendices
In the Field	26.4.18	—	D.G.O. visited D.H.Q. re gas-shelling of Don Front and Islonge Dump & re disposal of gassed clothing. C.C.A and D.G.O. visited 8/MO re supply of Iresh clothing for gassed cases and distribution of Vaseline. Visited 34th F.A. of Altride of Lime. Routine work by Batt R.G.Os. re number of gassed men.	
	27.4.18		D.G.O. in search of suitable location for dealing with "Gassed clothing" & O.R. Pont des Briques selected as a convenient place and arrangements made for all gassed clothes to be delivered there. D.G.Os. reports re at the above location. Routine work and reports on Gas-shelling received from Batt. R.G.Os. Further Gas-shelling at various places in Fort de Nieppe.	
	28.4.18		C.C.A visited D.G.O. re "Gas shell" reports. Routine work by R.G.Os.	
	29.4.18		D.G.O. visited D.H.Q. and location for Gas Hut. Gassed clothing dumps on Canal ready for treatment C.C.A. and D.G.O. 52nd Division visited D.G.O. Further Gas-shelling on Aik Front. Routine work by Batt Gas R.G.Os.	
	30.4.18		D.G.O. visited Fort de Nieppe and D.N.O. "Gas Hut" cross road. D.G.O. of 52nd Division visited R.G.O. re training of several units of 52nd Division. C.C.A visited R.G.O. re "Gas shelling" at Alers and by Rele attached to 5 Divi. Routine work Gas R.C.Os.	

No. 7.

War Diary
of
5th Divl. Anti Gas School
for
Month of May 1918.

[signature]
Captain R.S.
5" D.G.O.

Army Form C. 2118.

WAR DIARY
or
INTELLIGENCE SUMMARY
(Erase heading not required.)

of 5th Divisional Anti Gas School

Instructions regarding War Diaries and Intelligence Summaries are contained in F. S. Regs., Part II. and the Staff Manual respectively. Title pages will be prepared in manuscript.

Place	Date	Hour	Summary of Events and Information	Remarks and references to Appendices
In the Field	1.5.18		D.G.O. lectured Officers N.C.O.s & men of 1st Bedfords & 1st Cheshires on "Mustard Gas". 52nd D.G.O. attached to 5th Div. for Instruction. C.C.A. visited D.G.O. Gas Hut in course of erection in Foret de Nieppe.	
	2.5.18		Further lectures given by 5th D.G.O. to 1st Norfolks and 16th R.W.R. Arrangements made for construction of units attached from 52nd Divn. Chemical Advisers, Army Corps, visited D.G.O.	
	3.5.18 to 5.5.18		52nd Batt. Pioneer Battalion, and two Field Coys R.E.s were lectured & drilled and tested their Respirators in Lachrymator. Lt Perham 16th R.W.R. reported to D.G.O. for duty as Assistant Gas Officer. Corps Chemical Adviser visited Gas Hut in Foret de Nieppe.	
	6.5.18		D.G.O. and Lutman proceeded to forward location in Foret de Nieppe. C.C.A. visited D.G.O. 96/3 Lgt Hockley promoted to U.K. on special leave. Inspection of S.B.R.s of Bdes H.Q.s. Routine work by Bde H.C.O.s.	
	7.5.18 & 9.5.18		D.G.O. visited 13th Bde H.Q., Salvage Dump, 13th Field Ambulance, 14th R.W.R. and Div. H.Q. 250 "Tunnelling Coy" 5th D.A.S./159 Labour Coy & 284 A.E. Coy; the preceding units were lectured and drilled and passed through lachrymator. "Assistant D.G.O. visited Corps School and drilled 3 and	
	10.5.18		D.G.O. visited areas J10, J11, J10d which had been Yellow Cross gas shelled. Prompt measures had been taken and many casualties prevented. Assistant D.G.O. lectured and drilled No 11 Balloon Coy and 421 Labour Coy. About 1300 Yellow Cross shells were fired on the Divl. area. Routine work by Bde H.C.O.s. visited 13 & 14 Field Ambulances.	
	11.5.18		D.G.O. perused a meeting of Divl Gas N.C.O.s at forward location and gave them all the recent information in Gas Warfare and would constructions as to their duties. Asst also visited 13 & 14 Field Ambulances, D.H.Q., A.D.M.S and Salvage Officer. Assistant D.G.O. visited 514 Battery in Gas shelling.	
	12.5.18 & 14.5.18		D.G.O. visited 126 Battery in Yellow Cross Gas shelling. 13 & 14 Field Ambs: re-gassed cases and informed the front of "Alert zone" wire treatds. Assistant D.G.O. visited 352 A.T. Coy, No. 4 Gas Supply Coy, 102 Labour Coy, 357 Rd Construction Coy, 130 Labour Coy, Yo Sect. A.A. Battery A.A. No. 4 Sect A.A. Battery 35th R.E. Parters from R.A. Battery and Labour Coys were drilled and passed through Gas chamber. 115th Bde R.F.A. commenced the changing of respirators.	
	15.5.18 & 16.5.18		D.G.O. visited areas reached by Norfolks, Cheshires, B507 and C.E.A., 121 Battery position, and C152 Battery position. All this visited the Field Supply Depot, 230 A.T.Coy, 25th M.A.Convoy, 33rd E.C.3.4.5.18, Section C.A. Lectures given and units drilled and passed through lachrymator. Lectures given to C152 Battery in Mustard Gas. Assistant D.G.O. Thro' from Caire to NEUFPRE & 600 Blue & Green Cross gas shells were fired on to J5, J6, J12.	

Army Form C. 2118.

WAR DIARY
or
INTELLIGENCE SUMMARY.
(Erase heading not required.)

5th Divisional Anti-Gas School

Place	Date	Hour	Summary of Events and Information	Remarks and references to Appendices
In the field	19.5.18		Lecture from 62nd A.T. Field Coy passed through Gas chamber. D.G.O. visited 1st Bn. H.Q. Passed through lachrymator to the line following units:— D.L.O.	
	20.5.18 to 23.5.18		D.G.O. visited 111 Field Amb. re gassed cases. Passed I.G., and visited the Bn. Lt. H. B. Knight and 2/Lt 20 Infantry re Gas. 115 B.O.C.A. and well lectured, drilled and Passed through chamber. C.C.A. visited Sanitary Section. 230 A.T.C. and 69 Sanitary Section. Also visited 51 C.C.S. re gassed cases and gas plaster. L Lays Parts & Balls. Battery began jack a much at gas from gas shell water. Routine work by Rob. N.C.O.s	
	24.5.18		D.G.O. visited A.D.M.S. re Label for the Unit Truck on account of abnormal Michael Gas shelling; 2 N.F.R. and 1st Norfolks re gas shelling of their trenches. Assisted D.G.O. Ireland edified the following units:— 14th O.O. detatchment at 2005, Blue & Yellow Cros fell on the following areas K7 K8 K13. K9 K13.	
	25.5.18		Bn. Ga. NCOs attended lectures given by R.B.O. at school. C.C. visited R.B.O. Annexe - D.G.O. visited 36 Labour Coy, 149 Labour Coy, 111 Field Amb., Turtle re lecture and 15 Fld Amb. Sgt Mackley reported to 21 Corps School.	
	26.5.18 to 29.5.18		D.G.O. visited 65 Field Amb. 95 Lab UKs, O.P Rcks re Labm. re HQ of 2nd Bn. Dublin Fus. re gas to Pattni R.E., and Battins 7 152 Bn. Assistant D.G.O. visited the following units:- 51 & C.C.S., 123 Labour Coy, 111 A.A. Section, 169 Labour Coy and 570 C.S. Lectures given were passed through Lachrymator. 700 Blue and Green. Eoroys fell on N7c. Washington Horn or Chateau Visited by Staff.	
	29.5.18 to 31.5.18		Further lectures given to Sections of 152 Blur by D.G.O. Bgg. Gas Int. D.E.S. visited D.G.O. and inspected funton at Fort de Nieppe. Asst. D.G.O. visited the following gas at Plastic Lectures from 10 O.M.S. detail with Yellow Cross. 350 Green & Yellow Cross gas shells fell in N3, N32 T35, T29. T30. Routine work by Rob. Gas NCOs.	

Vol 8

War Diary
of
5th Divl. Anti Gas School
for
Month of June 1918

Y Parham Lt
A/Captain R.E.
D. G. O.

WAR DIARY
INTELLIGENCE SUMMARY.
5th Dist. Anti Gas School

Army Form C. 2118.

Place	Date	Hour	Summary of Events and Information	Remarks and references to Appendices
In the Field	1.6.18	—	Meeting of Divl. Gas NCOs held at "Gas Hut." Latest information given and instructions issued by D.G.O. Lecture given to A/152 Bde R.F.A. by D.G.O. Assistant. D.G.O. visited the following Corps Units, and instructed them on Anti Gas Measures:- 36th Sanitary Section; 196 Labour Coy and 133 A.T. Coy. Reports sent to C.C.C.A. 100 Blue Cross Shells were fired on to J28/J29.	
	2.6.18		D.G.O. visited D.H.Q. of Stimbro Horse, and Lectured Relief Pilot Party for Rio Roma. D/1.99.3 visited and instructed the following Units:- 20th Battn Machine 194 Labour Coy and 345 Rd Construction Coy. Party of Portuguese troops lecture on cycle to workshops. D/1.99.0 visited Jl Survey's Party.	
	3.6.18		D.G.O. visited R.S.M.G. and stores and Large party from 194 Labour Coy paraded at Gas Hut and were drilled and passed through Gas Chamber. 1300 Blue & Yellow Gas Shells fell on Bus area.	
	4.6.18		D.G.O visited Dun. Heavy 13"/15"/9.6" Bde HR 16" Rw.R.V.10" Bomb and 87 Battery. C.C.O visited D.S.O.	
	7.6.18		D/1.R.S.O visited the following units: 194 Labour Coy, 3n5 Rd Construction Coy and 155 A.T. Coy through which 111 Labr Battery N.G.O paraded off Gas Hut and were drilled and passed through Gas Chamber. 200 Green Cross Gas Shells were fired on to J28, J34.	
	8.6.18		Meeting of Divl. Gas NCOS at Gas Hut. Lecture given by D.G.O. The Gun positions of 52 Battery + Bollon 119 Battery, A/15 Battery and 120 Battery were visited by D.G.O and NCOs. D/12.9.0 visited 111 Bollon Coy. 160 Green Cross Gas Shells fell near Battery positions J28. Nine casualties.	
	9.6.18 & 10.6.18		D.G.O. visited D/w.R.A.2 + 14 Siege Battery and 39 Bollon Coy. Notice Boards placed at theatre placed 500 Green Yellow + Yellow Cross were fired on to J8, J9, J27, J28, J29. 1 gas case. D/1.848 visited 13"+14"+12"+4.5" Field Ambce, Stimbro Horse placed 40 F.A. Report staff tools J3RS + 121 Battery which were reported to have been over for 40 hrs. Quite satisfactory. C.C.G.O visited D.G.O at Lopdll. they visited W. sieges Batty and fell. Ambulances. 300 Green + Yellow Cross were fired on to J23 J27 J28 J29.	
	11.6.18			

WAR DIARY

INTELLIGENCE SUMMARY

5 Divl. Anti Gas School

Army Form C. 2118.

Place	Date	Hour	Summary of Events and Information	Remarks and references to Appendices
In the Field	12.6.18 to 13.6.19	—	G.G.O visited D.C.L. Ist and L.R.C. re supply of Cloth Union Gloves. Lecture given to Relay Patrol party for Vra Ferne on Mustard Gas and Treatment of Shell Shock. a/1/5/0 introduced by C.O. and O.C. Special Coy R.E. 400 Blue, Green, & Yellow Cross Gas shell fell in areas J5 J23 J29 J30 J33.	
	14.6.18		G.G.O. visited Dir H.Q. and in company with G.S.O. II visited Divn. Reception Camp to make arrangements for hutting and testing casualty. Instruction given to Off. from Reception Camp. a/1/5/0 visited Batt. H.Q. Left Bde. and gave advice re- erection of Gas Proof shelters. Routine Work by Bde. N.C.Os.	
	15.6.18		D.G.O visited C.C.A in morning and proceeded on leave to U.K. in the evening. Lt. Barlow a/1/R.G.O during his absence. Weekly meeting of Divn. Gas N.C.Os held at Gas Hut. a/1/R.G.O gave lecture to N.C.Os.	
	16.6.18 to 20.6.18		C.C.A visited School and Group R.M.S.M Lambe. a/1/R.G.O visited the following units. 196 Land Drainage Coy; 955 Labour Coy; No. 3 Forestry Coy; 254 A.J. Coy; 159 Watson Coy; 149 Labour Coy 161th M Coy; Parties from 130 Labour Coy and 159 Labour Coy Banner at Gas Hut and were drilled and passed through Gas Chamber. Canadian Artillery Gas Officer visited D.G.O HQ at Strandro Htne completed. 200 Green and Blue Cross Gas shells were fired on the J J23 J30 K8c.	
	21.6.18		a.J.R.G.O visited R.E. J 279 Ly Construction Coy; No. 11 Balloon Coy and Divl. Reception Camp. Parties from 130 & 169 Labour Coys paraded at Gas Hut and were drilled and passed through lachrymator. Routine work at stores by Bde. N.C.Os.	
	22.6.18		Weekly meeting of Divl. Gas N.C.Os. Lecture given by a.P.M.O. re afterwards visited 95 Field A.R., 14, 4.15 Field Ambulances and No. 11 Balloon Coy.	

Army Form C. 2118.

WAR DIARY
or
INTELLIGENCE SUMMARY.
(Erase heading not required.)

5 Divl: Anti-Gas School

Instructions regarding War Diaries and Intelligence Summaries are contained in F.S. Regs., Part II. and the Staff Manual respectively. Title pages will be prepared in manuscript.

Place	Date	Hour	Summary of Events and Information	Remarks and references to Appendices
In the field	23.6.18		A.D.G.O. visited Railway Construction Coy and lectured drilled and passed through Gas Chamber Party from 196 Land Drainage Coy.	
	to		Lectured the personnel of the Coy.	
	24.6.18		Paraded at Gas Hut and were drilled and passed through Gas Chamber. Lecture given to relief patrol party for No Roma. Routine work at stores and Hq Beh. Gas Sqts. C.C.A. & forty ft samples of American nose clips O.B.B. visited Bayards, 1st D.C.L.I. & Bayards & by the line no gas frosting & Lowers field drawn.	
	25.6.18		A.D.G.O. visited the proper treatment of Skull-holes and Chloride of Lime. Lew Ube experiments on all arms which had been gas shelled the previous night and also visited by Pvk, and reports of Gas Shelling forwarded to C.C.A. and G.S.O.II. Col. Whitmore. Ptn. Hd. to report as undrsferting to Sgt Woodward. 2000 Yellow Cross were fired on to J21, J27, J28 J33 & J36. Sgt Hogan evacuated.	
	26.6.18		A.D.G.O. visited the following Battry positions which had again been gas-shelled D15 Battry, 52nd Battry & 119 Battry. He also visited C.R.A. re- Gas shelling - Sgt Woodward proceeded on leave and Sgt Blyth 1st Infants relief for duty in place of Sgt Hogan at 100 Yellow Cross were fired at J33.	
	27.6.18		Gassed Officers. Cases treated successfully with Chlorene. A.D.G.O. visited C.R.B's 5th R.E Batt H.Q. and 521 Field Coy R.E's Brig General & Staff of 13" Rel. lectured. War L.R.R.s in Gas chamber. Sgt Jones 12 "Glos. proceeded on leave. 20.0 Yellow Cross Gas shells fired on and J51 to J58.	
	28.6.18		O.D.G.O. convened weekly meeting of Div. Gas N.C.O.s. Lecture given on recent funds. He visited Advance HQ of 13 495 7 Feld MA and agreed on protection of Pelt horses. Etc. Consulted also on the question of protecting Feld Ovenis Reports & Gas returns and C.O. Routine work at stores and Hq Div Gas N.C.O.s.	

F.B. Mayell Captain
5.A.D.O.

War Diary
of
5th Divl. Anti-Gas School.
for
Month of July 1916

G. Statham Lt. R.E.
D.S.O.

Army Form C. 2118.

WAR DIARY
or
INTELLIGENCE SUMMARY
(Erase heading not required.)

of 5th Divl. Gas Officer

Instructions regarding War Diaries and Intelligence Summaries are contained in F. S. Regs., Part II. and the Staff Manual respectively. Title pages will be prepared in manuscript.

Place	Date	Hour	Summary of Events and Information	Remarks and references to Appendices
In the Field	1.7.18	—	Acting D.G.O visited Div: H.Q., Divl. Reception Camp, D.G.O. 74th Divn: and Corps Chemical Adviser. Lecture on "Mustard Gas and method of treating shell holes" given to patrol party for Via Roma. Specimen dug-out entrance completed at Gas Hut, and Allied Gas: Clothing sent to Salvage. Routine work at stores and by Bde. Gas N.C.O.s.	
	2.7.18			
"	3.7.18		A/D.G.O visited all areas which had been subjected to Gas shelling and supervised the treatment and filling in of Shell Holes. Reports re gas shelling sent to G.S.O. II. and C.C.A. A quantity of Machine Gun Drums and Carriers were treated successfully with Chlorine. Routine work at stores and by Bde. Gas N.C.O.s. 1200 Yellow Cross gas shells were fired on to the following areas J9, J10, J15, J21, J22. No 505/26 Sgt Lees, 59 Divl Gas N.C.O. reported to 1A/D.G.O. and received instructions. Report received from No. 8 Red Cross Hospital that Capt. Greenwood R.B. 5 D.G.O had been admitted into Hospital.	
	5.7.18			
"	6.7.18		A/D.G.O. visited Divl.HQrs., 13th, 15th & 95th Bat.H.Q., 13th & 15th Field Ambs., 1st Cheshires, and Wagon Lines of C/296 & D/296 Bdes.R.F.A. Various reports and returns sent to G.S.O. II. and C.C.A. Army & Corps. Gas visited A/D.G.O. Routine work at Stores and by Bde. Gas N.C.O.s Eyepieces changed for C/296 & D/296 Bde R.F.A and for portion (200) of Divl Reserve.	
	12.7.18			
	13.7.19		A/D.G.O. visited Div H.Qrs., Divl. Reception Camp, 16th "Platt and 13th "Field Amb., Weekly meeting of Divl Gas NCOs held at Gas Hut. Various reports and returns rendered to G offices + C.C.A. Routine work at stores and by Div. Gas N.C.O.s. C.C.A. visited A/D.G.O.	
	16.7.18			
	17.7.18	—	Army + Corps N.C.O.s visited A/D.G.O. Various subjects discussed and defence scheme examined and criticized. Visits paid to E/15 Battery, 119 Battery and Via Roma. Routine work at stores and by Bde. NCOs.	

Army Form C. 2118.

WAR DIARY
INTELLIGENCE SUMMARY
(Erase heading not required.) of 5th Divl. Gas Officer.

Instructions regarding War Diaries and Intelligence Summaries are contained in F. S. Regs., Part II. and the Staff Manual respectively. Title pages will be prepared in manuscript.

Place	Date	Hour	Summary of Events and Information	Remarks and references to Appendices
In the field	18.7.18		A.D.G.O. visited Divn. H.Qrs. and A.D.M.S. Supply of P.D. clothing and treatment of gassed clothing discussed. Routine work at stores and by Bde. Gas N.C.Os.	
"	19.7.18		Official intimation received of the promotion of Capt. B.S.M. Evermoved R.B. to Commandant IV Corps Gas School, and of the appointment of Lt. F.D. Bonham, 16th R.W.R., to D.G.O. and to be transferred to R.B.S. Routine work at stores and by Bde. N.C.Os. Sgt. Woodward returned from leave.	
"	20.7.18		Weekly meeting of Divl. Gas N.C.Os. held at Gas Stat. Lecture given by D.G.O. Various reports rendered to "G" Office and C.C.A. Capt. B.S.M. Evermoved R.B. evacuated to England, Sick.	
"	21.7.18 to 25.7.18		D.G.O. visited Divn. H.Q., all Batteries of 59th Brun. R.F.A., 16th R.W.R., D15 Battery, 52nd Battery and Stores. Routine work at stores & by Bde. Gas N.C.Os. No.145.22 Sgt. Jones L.J. 12th Gloster evacuated to No.2 Australian C.C.S. 24.7.18. Sgt. Mayos returned from leave.	
"	26.7.18		D.G.O. visited all areas which had been gas-shelled and superintended the treating of shell holes. Reports re gas-shelling sent to "G" Office & C.C.A. Routine work at stores and by Bde. Gas N.C.Os. About 400 Yellow & Green Cross Gas-shells fell in J.21.	
"	27.7.18 to 28.8.18		Weekly meeting of Divl. Gas N.C.Os. held at Gas Stat. Lecture given by D.G.O. Various reports and returns for't to "G" Office and to C.C.A. Sgts. Hockley and Barton from Corps Gas School, attached for a fortnight's tour of duty with Bde. Gas N.C.Os. Routine work at stores and by Bde. Gas N.C.Os.	

WAR DIARY
or
INTELLIGENCE SUMMARY.
(Erase heading not required.)

Army Form C. 2118.

of 5th Divl. Gas Officer

Place	Date	Hour	Summary of Events and Information	Remarks and references to Appendices
In the field	29/7/18 to 30/7/18		D.G.O. visited 2nd KOSBs, 1st Rifle Bde, 1st R.W.R, 1st Devons and Gun positions of 59th Bde Artillery. Lectures given to Relief Party. C.C.A. visited D.G.O. and together they visited Battalion HQs and various Salt Bags. Horting Wood at intervals and by Blue Cross Trees. One hundred Green Cross and Blue Cross Gas shells fell in T9, T38.	
"	31/7/18		D.G.O. visited Divl. H.Q., stores and all Gas shelled areas. Lfts Hockly and Barton attached for two days to Divl. Artillery. Routine work by Divl Gas NCOs and at stables. Five hundred Yellow Cross Gas shells were fired on to T1, T5, T33, T35, T27, T26.	

L. Arlen Lt. R.E.
D.G.O.

Vol 10

War Diary
of
5th Divl. Gas Officer
for
Month of August 1918.

G. Barklamb Lt.
G.S.O.

Army Form C. 2118.

WAR DIARY
INTELLIGENCE SUMMARY.
(Erase heading not required.)

of 5th Cdn. Anti-Gas School

Place	Date	Hour	Summary of Events and Information	Remarks and references to Appendices
In the Field	1.8.18 to 2.8.18	—	D.G.O visited areas which had been subjected to Gas shelling and supervised proper treatment and filling in of Shell holes. Stenciled Horns issued to various units and fixed by Gas NCOs. Routine Work at Stores and by Res Gas NCOs. 200 Yellow and Green Cross Gas Shells were fired on to areas P5, J78d & J74d.	
"	3.8.18		Meeting of Div. Gas NCOs held at Gas Hut. Lecture given to NCOs by R.S.O on latest developments in Gas Warfare. Reports and returns sent to N.C.O and "E" offices.	
"	4.8.18		D.G.O visited all areas which had been Gas shelled and sent reports to G officer and A.C.Q. 600 Yellow and Green Cross Gas shells were fired on to areas J34, J39, J30 & R15.	
"	5.8.18		C.C.Q visited R.G.O and together they visited all Field Ambulances and various areas which had been gas shelled the previous day. D.G.O 61st Div. visited 5th C.G.O and took over stores etc. Res Gas NCOs landed over to enemy Res Gas NCOs of 61st Div. Lt Adam J. F., 16 Cdn I.R. reported to R.S.O and assumed duties of Assistant D.G.O.	
"	6.8.18		R.G.O and A/R.G.O visited all Gas shelled areas, and handed over hats and attrinske affects to 61st D.G.O.	
"			Move from WIDDEBROUCQ to WARDRECQUES. R.G.O visited C.C.Q and Ga H.Q.	
"	7.8.18			
"	8.8.18 to 9.8.18		A.G.O visited Corps Gas School MAMETZ, and C.C.Q. A.R.G.O visited all infantry Bde HQrs. Routine Work at Stores and by Res Gas NCOs.	

WAR DIARY
or
INTELLIGENCE SUMMARY.
(Erase heading not required.)

Army Form C. 2118.

Instructions regarding War Diaries and Intelligence Summaries are contained in F. S. Regs., Part II. and the Staff Manual respectively. Title pages will be prepared in manuscript.

Place	Date	Hour	Summary of Events and Information	Remarks and references to Appendices
In the Field	10.8.18		D.A.D.O. proceeded on leave to U.K. Lt. Adam I/c A.S.N. assumed the duties of D.A.D.O. in his absence.	
	11.8.18 to 12.8.18		A.D.O. visited C.C.O., Div. A.D.Os and 13th and 15th Bde HQrs. Arrangements made for training units whilst at rest. Routine work at Bdes and stores by N.C.Os.	
	14.8.18		Move from WARDRECQUES to FREVENT.	
	15.8.18 to 18.5.18		A.D.O. visited VI Corps C.A., Dis. A., C.R.A. and 27th Bde R.F.A. and made arrangements to give a series of lectures to Artillery units. Arrangements also made to instruct the firing of Stokes Mortars for Artillery and M.G. Battalion. No 6626 Gr. N. Lyons 2nd M.G. Bn. reported ECH.18.5.O for duty as instructor to Stokes charging party. About 800 officers were changed in drill by units.	
	19.5.18		Move from FREVENT to AUTHIE. Nominal Roll sent to C.C.O. IV Corps.	
	20.8.18		A.D.O. visited C.C.O. IV Corps. L.22995 "A" Gr. Hood, 5" R.G.O. returned to his unit. No 191319 Gr. Taylor S.M. S.R.G.O. reported to A.D.G.O. ex. L.Gt. Hart.	
	21.8.18		A.D.G.O. visited advanced Rnf. HQrs and afterwards investigated reported Gas Shelling of BUCQUOY. About 500 Blue Cross Gas shells were fired on to BUCQUOY, PUISIEUX & L.29.	
	25.8.18 to 25.8.18		A.D.G.O. visited Div. HQrs, and 13th, 95th + 15th Bde HQrs. Instructions given to Bde Gas N.C.Os re Gas shell reports. Routine work at stores and by Bde Gas N.C.Os.	

Army Form C. 2118.

WAR DIARY
or
INTELLIGENCE SUMMARY.
(Erase heading not required.)

Instructions regarding War Diaries and Intelligence Summaries are contained in F. S. Regs., Part II. and the Staff Manual respectively. Title pages will be prepared in manuscript.

Place	Date	Hour	Summary of Events and Information	Remarks and references to Appendices
In the Field	26.8.18	—	A.D.G.O. proceeded to FONQUEVILLERS. Lt Borlam returned from leave.	
" " "	27.8.18	—	Lt Borlam proceeded to FONQUEVILLERS and afterwards visited Div.H.Qrs. and Bde H.Qrs. A.D.G.O. visited 13th 15th & 95th Bde H.Qrs.	
" " "	28.8.18	—	Stores moved from AUTHIE to FONQUEVILLERS. A.D.G.O visited C.C.O and Divl Reception Camp, and made arrangements for training of drafts. Sgt McIntyre attached to Divl Reception Camp temporarily. A.D.G.O visited all Salvage Dumps and inspected Salved Arms gas appliances. A.D.G.O. proceeded to Captain in the Corps? R.F.S.	
" " "	29.8.18	—	A.G.O visited Divl. Reinforcement Camp in morning and C.R.A. and Salvage Dumps in afternoon. A.D.G.O. supervised training of drafts at Divl. Reinforcement Camp. Party from Divl. Reception Camp reported at 1 Gas School and were fitted with S.B.Rs. All S.B.Rs at Salvage Dumps were inspected and Blown appliances Salved.	
" " "	30.8.18	—	A.G.O visited all Salvage dumps in forward area. A.D.G.O attended Divl: Reinforcement Camp. Salved Work at Stores and by Bde HQrs.	
" " "	31.8.18	—	A.D.G.O proceeded to ACHIET LE GRAND to find suitable broken for stores supper and visited advance Div.HQrs. A.D.I.O. visited Corps C.O. re Gold Union.	

F.R. Oxland Capt. R.E.
A.D.G.O

War Diary
of
5th Divl. Anti Gas School
for
Month of September 1918.

F. Stephens Capt R.E.
S.G.O.

WAR DIARY
INTELLIGENCE SUMMARY

Army Form C. 2118.

(Erase heading not required.) of 5th Divl: Anti Gas School.

Instructions regarding War Diaries and Intelligence Summaries are contained in F.S. Regs., Part II. and the Staff Manual respectively. Title pages will be prepared in manuscript.

Place	Date	Hour	Summary of Events and Information	Remarks and references to Appendices
In the Field	1.9.18		Move from FONQUEVILLERS to ACHIET LE PETIT. D.G.O visited all Bde HQts. Routine work at stores and by Bde NCOs. 200 Yellow Cross Gas shells were fired on to the divisional front.	
"	2.9.18		D.G.O visited advanced Divl. H.Qts in morning and C.C.A and Divl Reception Camp in the afternoon. A small stock of SBRs also taken by A.D.G.O to Divl Reception Camp to be used for changing defective SBRs of drafts.	
"	3.9.18		C.C.A visited D.G.O. D.G.O visited SAPIGNIES and BAPAUME to inspect German Gas shell dumps. D.G.O visited dumps at BEUGNY and FAVREUIL, and Divl Salvage Arrangements made to inspect all salved Gas material at Divl Salvage dumps. 200 Yellow and Green Cross gas shells were fired on to divisional front.	
"	4.9.18			
"	5.9.18		D.G.O visited C.C.A and discussed various questions. He afterwards visited 5"T.G.Battn and arranged for the training of T.G personnel to fit new eyepieces and then visited all Bde HQts, arranging that the inspection of units by the Bde N.C.O's. A.D.G.O visited Divl. Reception Camp and arranged for the withdrawal of N.C.O to supervise the changing of eyepieces of the 5" Th. G. Battn. Col. Hartley, A.D.G.S and A. 3rd army visited D.G.O. 100 Green Cross Gas shells were fired on to the Divl. front.	

Army Form C. 2118.

WAR DIARY
of
INTELLIGENCE SUMMARY.
(Erase heading not required.) of 5 Div Anti Gas School

Instructions regarding War Diaries and Intelligence Summaries are contained in F. S. Regs., Part II. and the Staff Manual respectively. Title pages will be prepared in manuscript.

Place	Date	Hour	Summary of Events and Information	Remarks and references to Appendices
In the Field	6.9.18 to		During this period, the D.B.O. and staff carried out a complete inspection of S.B.Rs. of the whole division less artillery units. A consolidated report was sent to C.C.A. and G.S.O.1 on the above inspection. The fitting of new trophic respirators to the remainder of the 5th M.G. Battalion was also commenced and completed. Two N.C.Os from the army Gas school were attached to the R.G.O for instruction. C.C.A., Div HQrs, Bde HQrs and all unit HQrs were visited by the R.G.O and A.D.G.O visited Div Reception Camp. Routine work at stores and daily inspection of salved material.	
	15.9.18			
"	14.9.18		R.G.O visited C.C.A. A box of 12 containers was sent to Army C.A. for testing purposes. Two hundred S.B.Rs. were obtained from IV Corps troops owing to shortage.	
"	15.9.18 to 16.9.18		R.G.O and staff moved to BANCOURT. Reports based on the recent inspection of S.B.Rs in the division were despatched to 'G' 'Q' offices. These suggested:- 1. That periodical inspections by units were still lacking in thoroughness. 2. That containers were not demanded when necessary. 3. That serviceable S.B.Rs were not being returned.	
"	17.9.18 to 19.9.18		R.G.O visited C.C.A., 95th Bde HQ, Div HQ, C.R.E., and Bde HQrs. 91st Bde HQrs. Reception Camp and investigated reported Gas shelling of all kinds from all parts of the front. As a result of his investigations he found that about 250 Blue Cross and Yellow Cross Gas shells had been fired onto the Divl. front, and that the casualties totalled 13. A N.C.O reported for duty to the Divl. Reception Camp.	
	20.9.18 & 21.9.18		A.D.G.O visited C.C.A., Div HQ, C.R.A. and Divl. Reception Camp. A.D.G.O. visited main dressing station and forward areas. 15 Bde HQ, R.E. dump, and 13 Bde HQ. Routine work at stores and by Bde Gas N.C.Os.	
"	22.9.18		R.G.O visited HQrs 15th Bde HQrs and issued instructions to Bde N.C.O rs. Gas shell reports. Gas N.C.Os returned to their HQrs. A.D.G.O visited C.C.A. and took a supply of Army Gas NCO to Gas NCO at Div Reception Camp. Lethyrinator to Gas NCO at Divl. Reception Camp.	

Army Form C. 2118.

WAR DIARY
or
INTELLIGENCE SUMMARY.
(Erase heading not required.)

of 5th Divl. Anti-Gas School

Instructions regarding War Diaries and Intelligence Summaries are contained in F. S. Regs., Part II. and the Staff Manual respectively. Title pages will be prepared in manuscript.

Place	Date	Hour	Summary of Events and Information	Remarks and references to Appendices
In the Field	23.9.18		D.G.O visited 15th Bde. H.Q. 15th Field Ambulance and 13th S.A.D. He also discussed the following points with Staff. 1. Supply of chlorine of lime and formation of dumps. 2. Supply by Kerosinate of soda. 3. Supply by S.B. Arthys. for Anti Gas purposes.	
	to		A.D.G.O. visited Divl. Reception Camp, and D.D.M.S., and main dressing station daily re Gas casualties. Routine work at stores and by Bde. N.C.Os. Salvage dump visited daily and salved anti gas appliances inspected. During this period 450 Green, Blue and Yellow Cross Gas shells were fired on to Divl. front.	
	27.9.18		C.C.A. visited D.G.O. reported heavy Yellow Cross Gas shelling on divl. front. D.G.O. proceeded to forward areas and found that about 200 Yellow Cross and 200 Blue Cross Gas shells had been fired on to divl. area. He visited Divl. H.Q., 13th Bde H.Q. and main dressing stations and afterwards went report to C.C.A. and "G" staff.	
	28.9.18		A.D.G.O. visited main dressing station and Divl. Reception Camp. Various reports returns rendered to C.C.A. and Divl. H.Q.s]	
"	29.9.18		D.G.O. moving from BANCOURT to YTRES. Stores moved to BUS. Visit paid to Divl. H.Q. and dressing stations. Routine work at stores and by Bde. N.C.Os. 200 Blue Cross Gas shells were fired on to Divl. front.	
"	30.9.18		D.G.O. moved from YTRES to BUS. Investigation made of circumstances leading up to excessive casualties from 50 Yellow Cross Gas shells, and full reports sent to C.C.A. and D. officer. A.D.G.O. visited Divl. Reception Camp and inspected S.B.R's. Routine work at stores and by Bde. N.C.Os.	

F. Horlock Capt. R.E.
D.G.O.

68/12

War Diary
of
Gas Services 5th Division
for
Month of October 1918

F J Stokham Captain
D.G.O.

WAR DIARY
INTELLIGENCE SUMMARY.

(Erase heading not required.)

Army Form C. 2118.

of Gas Services 3rd Army

Place	Date	Hour	Summary of Events and Information	Remarks and references to Appendices
In the Field	7.10.18		D.G.O. handed over to 3rd Army Gas Officer and visited the following H.Qtrs. and Units:- Div.H.Q. 13th + 95th Bde. H.G., Rest Reception Camp and 5 W.R. Battalion. A.G.P.O. visited Rest Reception Camp daily, and Routine work at almost at Bde Gas R.O.O.S.	
	6		supervised the training of "drafts" and casuals passing through Camp.	
	8.10.18		The following officers were appointed "Gas Officers" to Artillery and Infantry Bdes:-	
			1. Lt. M.O. Allbert) Artillery Gas Officers	
			2. Lt. J.G. Vaughan) 5th D.A.C.	
			3. Lt. J. Griffiths) 13th Bde.	
			4. Lt. V.E. Weale) 16th R.H.A.	
			1st Norfolks	
			1st E. Surreys	
			15 Infantry Bde.	
			95 " "	
	9.10.18		A.G.O. visited 5 W.G. Battalion re changes of officers and 1st Norfolks. A.G.O. visited Rest Reception	
			Camp - No 6099 Sgt. BECK S., 1st Norfolks transferred to Gas Services.	
			D.G.O. convened a meeting for Bde. Artillery Gas Officers and N.C.O.S., at which latest developments	
	8.10.18		in Gas Warfare were discussed. Routine Work at Rest Reception Camp. Bdes. and stores.	
	9.10.18		No 43225 A/Sgt. HOGARTH T.W. reverted rank strength of Gas Services 3rd Army. D.G.O. visited Corps C.O. Bdes, A 6th	
			and Rest Reception Camp. Instructions issued to Bde. & Artillery Gas Officers re Gas shell reports reviews.	
	10.10.18			
	11.10.18		Move from BUS to GOUZEAUCOURT.	

Army Form C. 2118.

WAR DIARY
or
INTELLIGENCE SUMMARY.
(Erase heading not required.)

Army Gas Services 5th Division

Instructions regarding War Diaries and Intelligence Summaries are contained in F.S. Regs., Part II. and the Staff Manual respectively. Title pages will be prepared in manuscript.

Place	Date	Hour	Summary of Events and Information	Remarks and references to Appendices
In Field	12.10.18		D.G.O. and A/S.G.O. moved on to CAUDREY. Location returns rendered to C.I.O. "E" & "Q". Routine work at stores. Box respirators insp, and by Bde. Gas Reps.	
"	13.10.18		Arrangements made by D.G.O. to exchange all containers with aerial number below 100. A supply of containers was sent on to CAUDREY from stores for this purpose. L.G.O. visited 15th Bde H.Q's and 1st Norfolks.	
"	14.10.18		D.G.O. visited areas that had been subjected to gas shelling, BUSIGNIES, A.D.S. and 13th Bde M.R.S., C.C.S. called and wished an investigation made of German anti Gas attn at CAUDREY. This was carried out by L.G.O. and A/S.G.O. Several villages were searched by A.S.G.O. in order to locate any Gas-shell dumps. About 80 enemy Gas shells fell on T.8.	
"	15.10.18		Extensive Gas shelling reported on div. front. The area was investigated by D.G.O. and reports sent to C.C.A. and 6th Bde. offrs. 13th Bde drew a supply of allards of lime and Bleaching Lime. Casualties only were reported. From 2000 Blue and Yellow Cross Gas shells. Ful. wrecks 1st E. Lancy. Rpt'd to D.G.O. for duty at Batt. Reception Camp. Conference of St. Ors held at C.C.C. officers which 5th G.S.O. attended. About 20 Green Cross Gas shells fell in T.10 T.16, T.11. Routine search at stores and by Bde Gas Reps.	
"	16.10.18		D.G.O. visited all areas which had been subjected to Gas shelling and reported on. He also inspected salient anti gas appliances or salvage dump and at German Gas stores, to supply of Bleachant at Beds. area. Additional anti Gas P.S. clothing C.C.A. and general stores and Batt Reception Camp. 250 Blue, Green & Yellow Cross Gas shells were typed on the divisional front.	

WAR DIARY
INTELLIGENCE SUMMARY.

Army Form C. 2118.

of _Geo. Ross_ _5th Division_

Place	Date	Hour	Summary of Events and Information	Remarks and references to Appendices
L.M. Hall	21.10.18 to 23.10.18		Further slight gas shelling was reported and D.A.D.O. proceeded to investigate. He also visited D.H.Q. and 95th Bde. Also A.R.D.O. visited Div. Reception Camp. Stores moved from GOUZEAUCOURT to CAUDREY. Routine work by Bde. ROs.	
	24.10.18 to 25.10.18		D.O. visited stores and Dumps. A supply of "Mustard Gas" was obtained by D.A.D.O. to ROs at Div. Reception Camp for use in training drafts etc. A Ref. O. visits C.C.S. Routine work at stores and by Bde. Geo. ROs.	
	25.10.18 to 26.10.18		Bde. and Artillery Gas Officers and ROs met at B.H.Qs. for latest information. D.A.D.O. was empowered to and will make arrangements by D.A.D.O. to inspect all SBRs throughout Division. Special attention being given to Artillery Units. Canisters with approx number below 100 was withdrawn and others issued.	
	27.10.18 to 31.10.18		During the period events embracing 75 B.H.Qs. Bdes. attended "Gas Hut" in CAUDREY and were lectured, tested and passed through "Lachrymator." The percentage of various objects in SBRs of units was not high but numerous slight differences were noted. The standard of drill was generally fairly Good. Best was in no case really brilliant. The 16th Bat. R.W.K. als Eng. Company from the 1st Australia also passed at "Gas Hut" and were similarly dealt with. Routine work at stores and by Bde. Geo. ROs.	

L. Nolan Capt. R.E.
D.G.O.

W.D./3

War Diary
of
Gas Services 5th Divn:
for
Month of November 1918.

J. Stephen Captain R.E.
D.G.O.

Army Form C. 2118.

WAR DIARY
or
INTELLIGENCE SUMMARY
(Erase heading not required.)

of Gas Services 5th Divn.

Place	Date	Hour	Summary of Events and Information	Remarks and references to Appendices
In the Field	1.11.18 to 3.11.18		The following units paraded at "Gas Chamber" and were lectured, drilled and passed through lachrymator. 2nd L.O.S.Bs, 13th T.M.Batty, 1st R.W.Kents, 527 Field Coy R.Es, and 5th R.E.Batt". Drill was Good throughout, and there were few defects. Reports were sent to C.C.R.E. G. Office and 'Q' Office. Routine work at stores and by Bde Gas N.C.Os.	
"	4.11.18		D.G.O. moved from CAUDREY to NEUVILLE. Lt Adam, assistant D.G.O, went to 1st Corps Gas School to assist Commandant. Stores remained at CAUDREY.	
"	5.11.16		D.G.O. took over from Gas Officer 32nd Divn and visited Divl H.Qtrs. Routine work at stores & by Bde Gas N.C.Os. Slight Gas shelling reported in Arty. front.	
"	6.11.18 to 7.11.18		Yellow Cross Gas shelling reported in FORET DE MORMAL. No casualties occurred. Visit paid to Divl H.Qtrs by D.G.O. Routine work at stores.	
"	8.11.18		D.G.O. moved to PONT SUR SAMBRE. Stores still remained at CAUDREY.	
"	9.11.16 to 10.11.16		D.G.O. visited Divl. and Bde HQrs, and area reported to have been Gas shelled. No casualties reported.	

Army Form C. 2118.

WAR DIARY
~~INTELLIGENCE SUMMARY.~~
(Erase heading not required.)

of Gas Services 5th Div.

Instructions regarding War Diaries and Intelligence Summaries are contained in F.S. Regs., Part II. and the Staff Manual respectively. Title pages will be prepared in manuscript.

Place	Date	Hour	Summary of Events and Information	Remarks and references to Appendices
In the Field	11.11.18		ARMISTICE from 11.00 hrs to-day. D.G.O moved from PONT SUR SAMBRE to JOLIMETZ.	
	12.11.18 to 13.11.18		Stimulo turns sent back to Base. D.G.O visited D.w.A.Q to and A.C.A. Routine work at stores.	
	14.11.18		Lt Adam, A.D.G.O. and his batman reported to 1/5 A.r.S.M. Routine work at stores.	
	15.11.18 to 19.11.18		Reserves of Anti Gas appliances returned to Base, with the exception of a few S.B.Rs for "immediate" replacements. Records and Files examined, and unnecessary papers destroyed.	
	20.11.18		D.G.O moved from JOLIMETZ to LE QUESNOY. Units continued to return their reserves, which were despatched to Base by stores personnel.	
	21.11.18		Nominal Rolls giving Regt. Nos:, Names, Rank, Regts and Civil occupations, sent to G.H.Q, 4th Army + 4th Corps.	
	22.11.18		D.G.O proceeded on leave to LE HAVRE.	

Army Form C. 2118.

WAR DIARY
or
INTELLIGENCE SUMMARY.
(Erase heading not required.) of Gas Services 5th Divn.

Place	Date	Hour	Summary of Events and Information	Remarks and references to Appendices
I. the Field	23.11.18		Various returns sent to C.C.A. & Q officer. 26079 A/ Book. S granted special leave to U.K.	
"	24.11.18 to 29.11.18		Stocktaking of stores. Surplus stores sent to Base. Travel made on Le Quesnoy for Indents for replacements of S.B.Rs.] suitable stores. Visits to various units re	
"	28.11.18		Stores moved from Caudrey to Le Quesnoy. Return rendered to C.C.A. IV Corps, of all Honours and Awards gained by Gas Services 5" Divn, during the war.	
"	29.11.18 to 30.11.18		S.B.Rs issued to various units to replace deficiencies. Also Respirators returned to stores by units.	

J Stoham Cpt R.E.
D.A.G.

Vol 14.

War Diary
of
Gas Services 5th Divn.
for
Month of December 1918.

G. Dehan Capt RE.
D.G.O.

Army Form C. 2118.

WAR DIARY
of
INTELLIGENCE SUMMARY of Gas Services 5th Div.
(Erase heading not required.)

Place	Date	Hour	Summary of Events and Information	Remarks and references to Appendices
In the Field	1.12.18		D.G.O. returned to LE QUESNOY from leave in France.	
"	2.12.18 to 4.12.18		Routine work at stores and by Bde. N.C.Os. Attached personnel of 206 Prot. Employment Coy. attended a Medical Board.	
"	5.12.18		No. 34029 Pte. Woodward A. 1st D.C.L.S. granted leave to the U.K. from 6.12.18 to 20.12.18.	
"	6.12.18 to 8.12.18		Routine work at stores and by Bde. N.C.Os. Horse Respirators withdrawn from Units and despatched to Base. Brigades moved from LE QUESNOY.	
"	14.12.18 & 15.12.18		D.G.O. moved from LE QUESNOY to SOUS-LES-BOIS.	
"	16.12.18		D.G.O. moved from SOUS-LES-BOIS to ERQUILINNES.	
"	17.12.18		Stores moved from LE QUESNOY to MANAGE.	

Army Form C. 2118.

WAR DIARY
or
INTELLIGENCE SUMMARY.
(Erase heading not required.)

of Gas Services 5th Div.

Instructions regarding War Diaries and Intelligence Summaries are contained in F. S. Regs., Part II. and the Staff Manual respectively. Title pages will be prepared in manuscript.

Place	Date	Hour	Summary of Events and Information	Remarks and references to Appendices
In the Field	18.12.18 to 20.12.18		D.G.O moved from ERQUILINNES to BINGHE and from BINGHE to NIVELLE.	
"	21.12.18		Stores moved from MANAGE to GEMBLOUX. D.G.O moved from NIVELLE to BAISNES.	
"	22.12.18 to 24.12.18		Routine work at Office, Stores, and by Bde N.C.Os. No.6079 Sgt Buck G. 1st Norfolks returned from leave. No. 34029 Pt Woodward A. 1st D.C.L.I. returned from leave to the U.K.	
"	25.12.18		XMAS DAY.	
"	26.12.18 to 31.12.18		Routine Work at Office & Stores & by Bde N.C.Os. A.F.s Z.16 completed and forwarded to Ministry of Labour.	

Y Stokes Capt OC

Vol 15

Confidential.

War Diary of :—

Gas Services.

Headquarters 5 Division.

January 1st 1919.

to

January 31st 1919.

L.V. Askew Captain R.E.
D.G.O. 5-Div.

Army Form C. 2118.

WAR DIARY
or
INTELLIGENCE SUMMARY.
(Erase heading not required.)

Instructions regarding War Diaries and Intelligence Summaries are contained in F. S. Regs., Part II. and the Staff Manual respectively. Title pages will be prepared in manuscript.

Place	Date	Hour	Summary of Events and Information	Remarks and references to Appendices
RHISNES	1.1.19		A.D.O. proceeded on leave to CARCASSONNE, FRANCE. Office work.	
do	2.1.19		Sunday. Return sent to Q. Office. Selecting certificate changed.	
do	3.1.19		A.W. Lamputt proceeded on leave to BRUSSELS for US LEAVE. Office work.	
do	4.1.19		A.W. Lamputt returned off leave ex BRUSSELS. Office work.	
do	6.1.19		A.W. Lamputt arrived Wheel. Motor car B.20 woodyard at B 28. Building being refitted to Q. Office garage.	
do	6.1.19		Instructions sent to 8th for A.D.O to know requirements of officers billets to cover leave in post. Sent to Q. Office. Returned to Q. Office.	
do	7.1.19		Instructions and Bicycle found. Officers M.L. returning to return to base. Bicycle No. B 40860 returned to L.B.S. office. O.C. 826 M.S.	
do	8.1.19		A.W. Lamputt to RHISNES to investigate situation. Dispersal area 15.1.19 notifying to Q. Office. Requirements to office.	
do	9.1.19		Orders received from G.H.Q. H.S. to demobilisation of N.Z. Larquice. All regiments to Q. Office.	
do	10.1.19		Office work.	
do	11.1.19		A.D.O. returning from leave to CARCASSONNE, FRANCE. Office work.	

Army Form C. 2118.

WAR DIARY
or
INTELLIGENCE SUMMARY.
(Erase heading not required.)

Instructions regarding War Diaries and Intelligence Summaries are contained in F. S. Regs., Part II. and the Staff Manual respectively. Title pages will be prepared in manuscript.

Place	Date	Hour	Summary of Events and Information	Remarks and references to Appendices
RHISNES	12.1.19		Lieut. proceeded to Loftus at Sembeux. Office work	
do	13.1.19		Lieut. Leuwers went to Liege. 16 Labourers went to C.O. I. Office for distribution. Office work.	
do	14.1.19		Lieut. visited D. Office. Refugees called at Office. Office work.	
do	15.1.19		Lieut. Col. Enjoro returned. Officers to discuss work with military authorities. Office work.	
do	16.1.19		Office work	
do	17.1.19		Various reports and returns sent to D. Office.	
do	18.1.19		Office work	
do	19.1.19		Office work. Letter to publishing dept. Exchange	
do	20.1.19		Office work	
do	21.1.19		Demob. and other returns to C.O. Office. Lieut. returned to Liege. War Office.	
do	21.1.19		Office work	
do	22.1.19		Received acknowledgment of Q.M.S.I. of S. ed. Languard. Office work.	

Army Form C. 2118.

WAR DIARY
or
INTELLIGENCE SUMMARY.
(Erase heading not required.)

Instructions regarding War Diaries and Intelligence Summaries are contained in F. S. Regs., Part II. and the Staff Manual respectively. Title pages will be prepared in manuscript.

Place	Date	Hour	Summary of Events and Information	Remarks and references to Appendices
RHISNES	23.1.19		Lieut. Wolahan A.V.C. arrived Divisional H.Q. at RHISNES. Officer ill.	
do	24.1.19		A.V.O. visited 16 Rue du Lion at LEUZE. A.V.O. attended Divisional Officer weekly report render D.D.V. Office. A.V.O. to BEMBOUX to see Div Cap.	
do	25.1.19		Lieut. & Sub. Officers weekly rendered. A.V.O. to hospital & report on officer's repast. No fresh. Officer ill.	
do	26.1.19		Officer ill.	
do	27.1.19		A.V.O. to proceed for demobilisation. Wrote reports opening statement to office. Little steps. Capt. R.A. appointed Officer illness.	
do	28.1.19		A.V.O. visited Divisional Office. Des. Dagley from V. Officer indewed situation reports received. Special R.E.J. Office ill.	
do	29.1.19		Weekly reports rendered.	
do	30.1.19		Dep. to LITTEAU & BEMBLOCK. Officer ill. & R.	
do	31.1.19		Officer ill.	

L.I. Wolahan Captain AVC
5 A.V.O.

Vol 16

War Diary
of
Gas Services. 5 Division.

From 1.2.19. to 26.2.19.

F.U. Askew. Capt. R.E.
D.G.O. 5 Div.

Army Form C. 2118.

WAR DIARY
or
INTELLIGENCE SUMMARY.
(Erase heading not required.)

Instructions regarding War Diaries and Intelligence Summaries are contained in F. S. Regs., Part II. and the Staff Manual respectively. Title pages will be prepared in manuscript.

Place	Date	Hour	Summary of Events and Information	Remarks and references to Appendices
RHISNES	1.2.19		Office work.	
"	2.2.19		D.A.O. proceeded on leave to U.K. Report at usual departure centre.	
"	3.2.19		Lt Menzies went to Rouen at Luncheon.	
"	4.2.19		Office work. Information received that Lt Menzies has been detached from this unit due to leave to U.K. at 8 A.M. & left again at 4 P.M. to rejoin unit via Rouen. Rue d'Espagne sent to G.O. II Corps.	
"	5.2.19		Office work.	
"	6.2.19		Office work.	
"	7.2.19		Office work. Weekly return rendered.	
"	8.2.19		Office work.	
"	9.2.19		Office work.	
"	10.2.19		Office work.	
"	11.2.19		Office work.	
"	12.2.19		Office work.	

Army Form C. 2118.

WAR DIARY
or
INTELLIGENCE SUMMARY.
(Erase heading not required.)

Instructions regarding War Diaries and Intelligence Summaries are contained in F. S. Regs., Part II. and the Staff Manual respectively. Title pages will be prepared in manuscript.

Place	Date	Hour	Summary of Events and Information	Remarks and references to Appendices
RHISNES	13.2.19		Office work. Sgt Birch proceeded to U.K. for demobilisation.	
"	14.2.19		Office work. Sgt Wenzie proceeded to U.K. for demobilisation.	
"	15.2.19		Office work.	
"	16.2.19		Office work.	
"	17.2.19		Office work.	
"	18.2.19		Office work.	
"	19.2.19		Office work.	
"	20.2.19		Office work. A/Lieut. Baker RE Shire, Sinclair Scard to ret. leave to Blighty. Capt is Ay. Bde. re Groundwires.	
"	21.2.19		Office work. Wrote reports and letters resn.	
"	22.2.19		Office work. Rec'd receipt of documents returned, 10pm. Office. A.D.O. to D. office.	
"	23.2.19		Office work 12. A.D.O. to Div. at Heinbaur.	
"	24.2.19		Office work.	

Army Form C. 2118.

WAR DIARY
or
INTELLIGENCE SUMMARY.
(Erase heading not required.)

Instructions regarding War Diaries and Intelligence Summaries are contained in F.S. Regs., Part II. and the Staff Manual respectively. Title pages will be prepared in manuscript.

Place	Date	Hour	Summary of Events and Information	Remarks and references to Appendices
RHISNES	25.2.19		Officework	
"	26.2.19		Officework	
"	27.2.19		Officework. D.y.D. to works at Jemiftine	
"	28.2.19		Officework. D.y.D. visited b.A. Jdury. Aburtts netwarks Return and report needed	

F.W. Adam Capt. R.E.
D.y.O. 5 Div.

Confidential.

War Diary.
———
of
———
Gas Services, 5 Division.

From 1st March 1919.
To 31st March 1919.

L. W. Askam. Captain R.E.
D.G.O. 5 Division.

Army Form C. 2118.

WAR DIARY
or
INTELLIGENCE SUMMARY.
(Erase heading not required.)

Instructions regarding War Diaries and Intelligence Summaries are contained in F. S. Regs., Part II. and the Staff Manual respectively. Title pages will be prepared in manuscript.

Place	Date	Hour	Summary of Events and Information	Remarks and references to Appendices
RHSNES	1. 3. 19.		O.C.O. called in to review Officers to Army officers work.	
"	2. 3. 19.		Office work. Letter received from G.O.C. IV Army re issue of officers offa service.	
"	3. 3. 19.		Office work. Reply to G.O.C. IV Army.	
"	4. 3. 19.		Office work.	
"	5. 3. 19.		Office work.	
"	6. 3. 19.		Office work.	
"	7. 3. 19.		Office work. Letter to Staff Capt. re issuing of radios to officers on duty. He did.	
"	8. 3. 19.		Office work.	
"	9. 3. 19.		Office work.	
"	10. 3. 19.		Office work. Letter to O officers re issue results of just bicycles	
"	11. 3. 19.		Office work. O.H.O. bicycles handed in to all R.T.O's at Havre D.D. to 2Als at perimeter.	

A7092. Wt. w188 9/M1293 750,000. 1/17. D. D. & L., Ltd. Forms/C2118/14.

Army Form C. 2118.

WAR DIARY
or
INTELLIGENCE SUMMARY.
(Erase heading not required.)

Instructions regarding War Diaries and Intelligence Summaries are contained in F. S. Regs., Part II and the Staff Manual respectively. Title pages will be prepared in manuscript.

Place	Date	Hour	Summary of Events and Information	Remarks and references to Appendices
RHISNES	12.3.	19	Officers R. Recived of [illeg] all the cycles been dealt with & bays.	
"	13.3.	19	Officers with. Recived letter from Staff for plain gas exercises & to demobilisation of officers.	
"	14.3.	19	Officers with. NIR went to RHQ at [illeg] receiving reports re: Urgent matters.	
"	15.3.	19	Officers work, Lett. plans & instructions for the disposal of Officers men & motor cycles.	
"	16.3.	19	Officers work.	
GEMBLOUX	17.3.	19	Officers work. Hd. moved to Gembloux.	
"	18.3.	19	Officers work. Continued with cycle courses ret to W. office	
"	19.3.	19	Officers work.	
"	20.3.	19	Officers work.	
"	21.3.	19	Officers work.	
"	22.3.	19	Officers work.	

Army Form C. 2118.

WAR DIARY
or
INTELLIGENCE SUMMARY.
(Erase heading not required.)

Instructions regarding War Diaries and Intelligence Summaries are contained in F. S. Regs., Part II. and the Staff Manual respectively. Title pages will be prepared in manuscript.

Place	Date	Hour	Summary of Events and Information	Remarks and references to Appendices
GEMBLOUX	23.3.19.		Office work.	
"	24.3.19.		Office work. Up to blancs Sablons to view lines.	
			Office work.	
"	25.3.19.			
"	26.3.19.		Office work. Up to Lawe to send R.E. Officers.	
			Office work.	
"	27.3.19.		Office work.	
"	28.3.19.		Office work. About to Laweretow, sending R.E. Officers dn.	
			Office work.	
"	29.3.19.		Office work.	
"	30.3.19.		Office work.	
"	31.3.19.		Office work.	

G.U. McLaue. Captain R.E.
C.R.E. 5 Division.

www.ingramcontent.com/pod-product-compliance
Lightning Source LLC
Chambersburg PA
CBHW081246170426
43191CB00037B/2061